First edition published in 2025 by Flying Eye Books Ltd.
27 Westgate Street, London, E8 3RL.

Illustrations © Ben Newman 2025

Scientific consultant: Alex Acklam

1 3 5 7 9 10 8 6 4 2

Text by Ben Elcomb
Edited by Christina Webb
Designed by Sarah Crookes

Published in the US by Flying Eye Books Ltd.

Printed in China on FSC® certified paper.

ISBN: 978-1-91312-324-6

www.flyingeyebooks.com

THE FAST LANE

BEN NEWMAN

FLYING EYE BOOKS

CONTENTS

WELCOME TO STEMVILLE

You've stumbled across one of the most amazing places there is to visit. Stemville is home to lots of weird and wonderful characters of all shapes and sizes. Most of the time the residents get along just fine, but occasionally sparks fly and there are disagreements and problems to solve. One thing's for sure, there's always something new to discover in this terrific town!

FROM TOWN TO TRACK

Stemville is a peaceful and calm place to live. But once a year it gets very busy and very loud! When the annual Big Race descends on the town, its streets are transformed into a Formula 1 racetrack. Most residents are happy to help get the town ready, temporarily closing roads, constructing barriers and building pit stops. Others are not too pleased, and complain about the traffic, road diversions, business closures – and the noise!

All about F1
There are many types of motor racing in the world, and Formula 1, or F1, is the highest class. F1 runs races called Grand Prix (French for 'big prize'), where teams work together to compete against each other.

Street circuits

Some races take place on circuits in stadiums, others on purpose-built road circuits, and some are on street circuits. Street circuits are on public roads that have been temporarily closed-off – just like Stemville will be for the Big Race.

Types of racing tracks

Stock
Specially modified cars racing on oval-shaped tracks and racecourses.

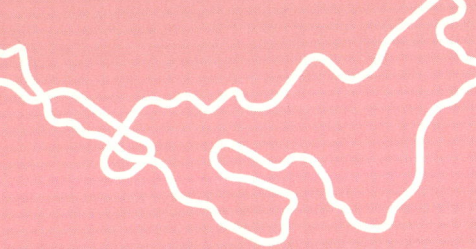

Rallying
Road or cross-country point-to-point courses, testing speed and navigation.

Indy 500
Race on a 2.5-mile permanent track for 200 laps, totalling 500 miles.

Drag
Two vehicles competing along a straight course.

11

FIERCE COMPETITORS

Meet Frankie, part of the Thunderfoot hare family of racing drivers who have lifted countless trophies since the Big Race began. The Thunderfoots have taken pole position for generations, and many believe Frankie to be the fastest driver yet! Her family won't accept anything less than first place, and she shares their ambition!

OUR RACE CAR IS LOOKING SHARP, AND I'M READY TO SHINE!

F1 cars are fast – really fast! They can achieve speeds of over 200 mph.

And here is Wilbur Hardshell. He and his family are an unlikely race team, tending to take the slow and steady approach to any situation. The Hardshell tortoises prefer to use their brainpower to solve problems, finding technical solutions rather than speedy shortcuts to succeed.

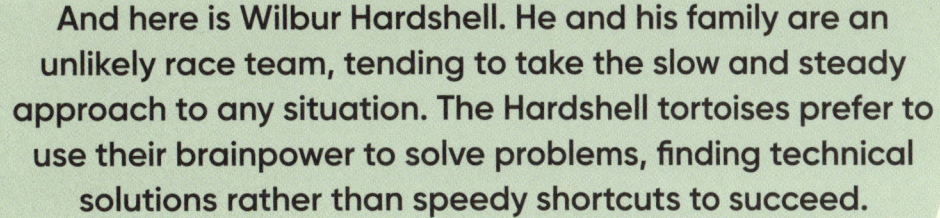

IT'S AS MUCH ABOUT THE SMARTS AS IT IS ABOUT THE PARTS!

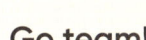

F1 cars are like rocket ships on wheels. They can accelerate from 0 to 60 miles per hour (mph) in just 2 seconds!

Go team!

F1 is not just about the driver – it's truly a team sport. Each team can be made up of over 600 people, including designers, engineers and mechanics.

RACING CARS

Each year, different types of cars compete in the Big Race. This year, it's Formula 1! Wilbur Hardshell's grandpa won the first and only trophy for the Hardshell family many years ago with an F1 racing car. Now it's Wilbur's turn to drive... But how could a tortoise beat a hare in a race?

There are two types of race car. Some have wheels outside the body (open-wheeled) and others have wheels below the body (closed-wheeled).

Closed-wheel race cars

Stock Car
Max speed: 200 mph

Stock cars are regular cars that have been powered up to race. They mostly compete on oval-shaped tracks.

Rally Car
Max speed: 140 mph

Rally cars are also improved regular cars, and race off-road on rough terrain. Because of this, they are not as fast.

Open-wheel race cars

Indy Car
Max speed: 240 mph

Popular in the USA, Indy cars race on oval-shaped circuits and road courses.

Drag Car
Max speed: 330 mph

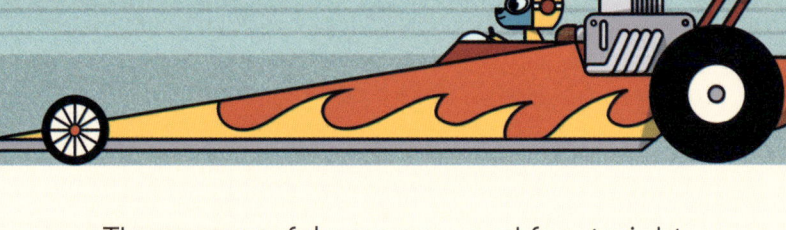

These powerful cars are used for straight short tracks because they're not so nifty with corners. Drag cars often need to release a parachute to slow down at the end of a race!

Formula 1
Max speed: 220 mph

This open-wheeler is the most famous type of race car.

The world's first official road race was won by a motor carriage. It averaged just 15 mph!

F1 Timeline
F1 officially began in 1950. The cars have changed a lot since then!

1950s
Narrow tyres, engine at front

1960s
Wider tyres, engine at back

1970s
Stronger aluminium chassis, wings added, air box for engine

1976
For a short while, six-wheeled F1 cars were built to give more grip for corners, with porthole windows for drivers to see the smaller front wheels

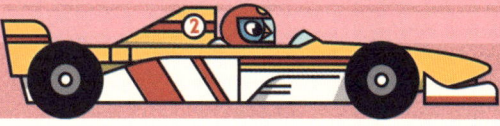

1980s
Front and rear tyres the same size, stronger and lighter carbon fibre chassis

1990s
More head protection, lower seats

2000s
Streamlined sides to cut through air faster

DESIGN, BUILD, TEST

Wilbur calls upon the best person he can think of to guide him through the dizzying world of race car construction – Grandpa Hardshell! They meet with a huge team of Hardshell designers and manufacturers ready to build the perfect race car... from scratch!

The word 'formula' in Formula 1 refers to the strict set of rules that the cars must meet so that they can be as evenly matched in a race as possible.

Some race car construction teams are made up of over 100 people!

Race car engines, or 'power units', are built both by hand and with machines.

Each race car is designed and built from scratch every year.

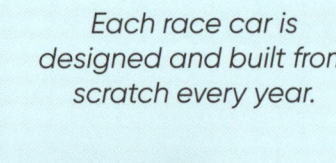

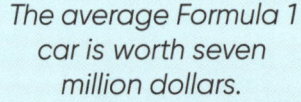

The average Formula 1 car is worth seven million dollars.

Computer-aided Design (CAD)

Designers and engineers create and test the cars on a computer before building them. This means engineers can test designs without making a car.

The body

The car bodies are built from a strong, lightweight material called carbon fibre, the same material used to make jumbo jets, which can be easily moulded into any shape.

Simulators

The drivers practise in simulators, which is like an immersive computer game that replicates how the real race will begin, so they can get a feel for the track.

Wind-tunnel testing

A smaller model car will run on a belt like a treadmill, while a huge turning fan blows strong winds from every angle to see how the car reacts at top speeds!

Shakedown

The teams test-drive the car. They ignite the engine, run the car on the track, check for any fuel leaks, practise speedy pit stops and check the tyres have the right amount of air in them.

HIGH-TECH CAR PARTS

Team Thunderfoot take one last walk around their car. And if they do say so themselves, it's looking more than ready. Shiny suspension coils? Check! Chassis with the latest Thunderfoot graphics? Check! Dazzling cockpit with cutting-edge safety features? Check and check!

Frankie is pleased with her bold custom-fitted full-body race suit, complete with Thunderfoot logo. She wants to look her best for her photo finish.

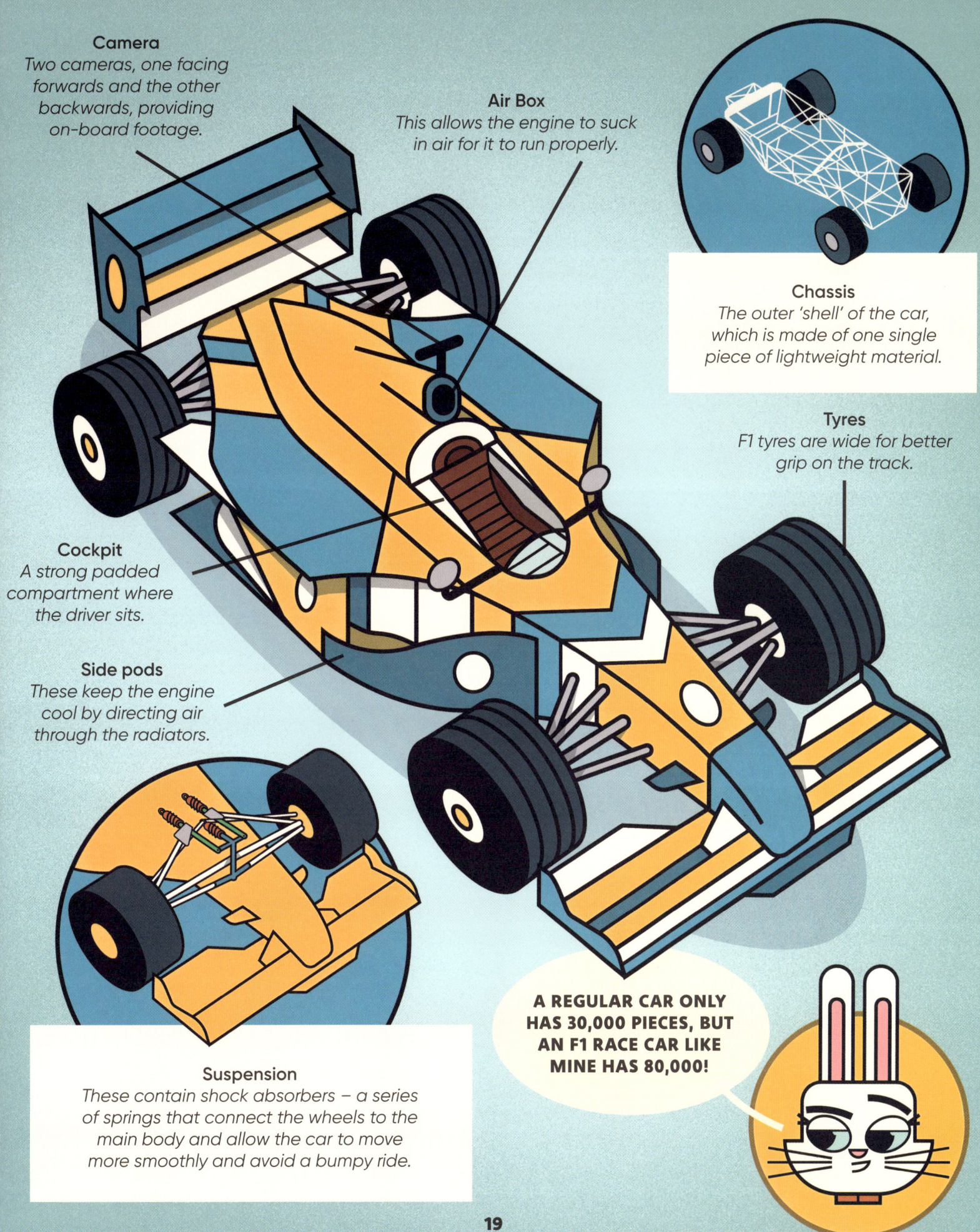

Camera
Two cameras, one facing forwards and the other backwards, providing on-board footage.

Air Box
This allows the engine to suck in air for it to run properly.

Chassis
The outer 'shell' of the car, which is made of one single piece of lightweight material.

Tyres
F1 tyres are wide for better grip on the track.

Cockpit
A strong padded compartment where the driver sits.

Side pods
These keep the engine cool by directing air through the radiators.

Suspension
These contain shock absorbers – a series of springs that connect the wheels to the main body and allow the car to move more smoothly and avoid a bumpy ride.

A REGULAR CAR ONLY HAS 30,000 PIECES, BUT AN F1 RACE CAR LIKE MINE HAS 80,000!

GIZMOS AND GADGETS

Frankie has a state-of-the-art helmet featuring a laser-etched emblem of the family's signature thunderbolt. Wilbur hopes Grandpa Hardshell's vintage helmet will bring him luck. He takes in advice from his family – he may be the one in the cockpit, but there's a whole team behind him.

Hang on, what are the Thunderfoots doing at the Hardshell garage? Rather than coming to intimidate the Hardshells, shouldn't they be making sure Frankie is race ready?

Suits

F1 drivers wear a full-body race suit made from fire-resistant materials.

Helmets

Each driver has their own custom-made carbon fibre helmet that supports their head and neck. It can deflect debris, withstand crashes, fire and extreme G-force.

Radio
The helmet has a microphone and earphones built into it, so the driver can communicate with their pit-stop team! This helps them make quick decisions, alert each other to any issues and discuss tactics during the race.

It can get very hot inside a cockpit – up to 60 degrees Celsius. Hotter than a hot summer's day!

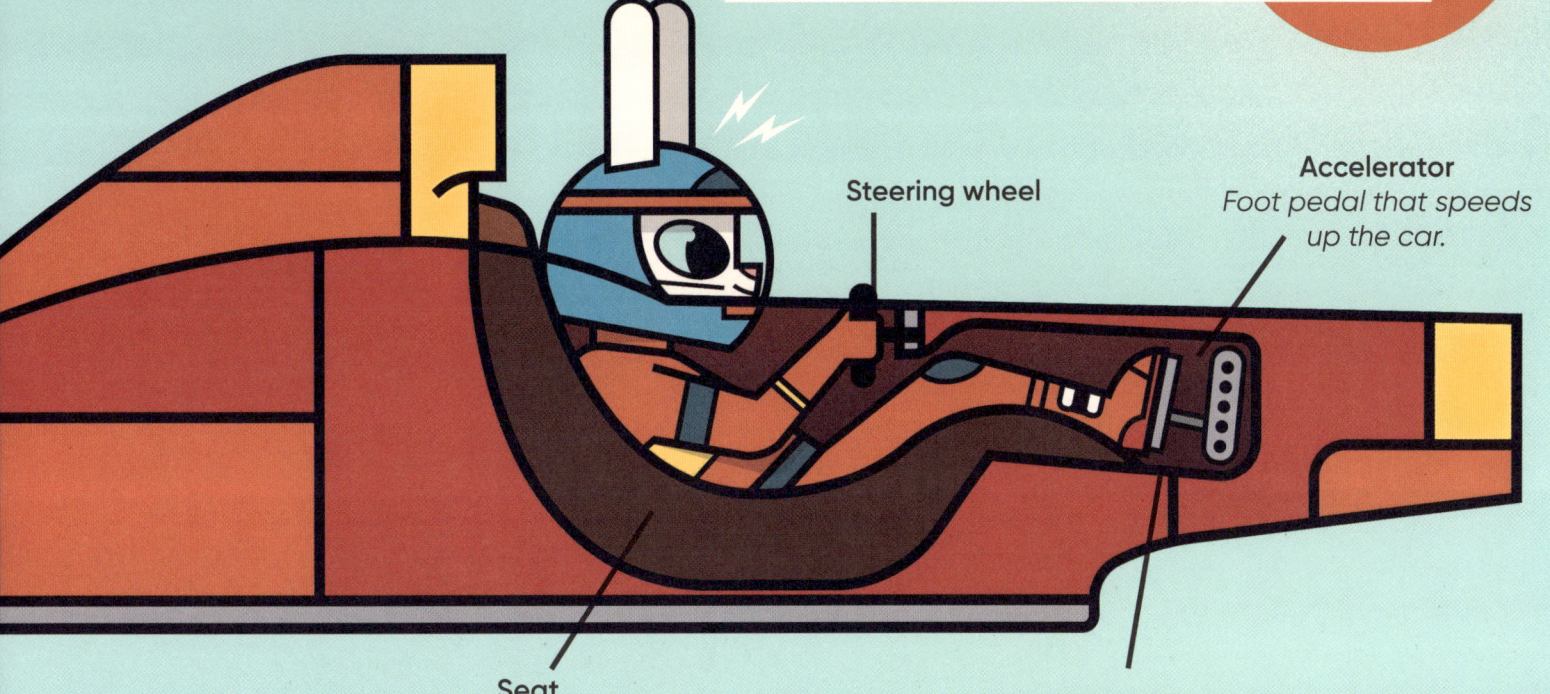

Steering wheel

Accelerator
Foot pedal that speeds up the car.

Seat
Made-to-measure for minimal movement and made of shock-resistant materials.

Brake
Foot pedal that slows the car down.

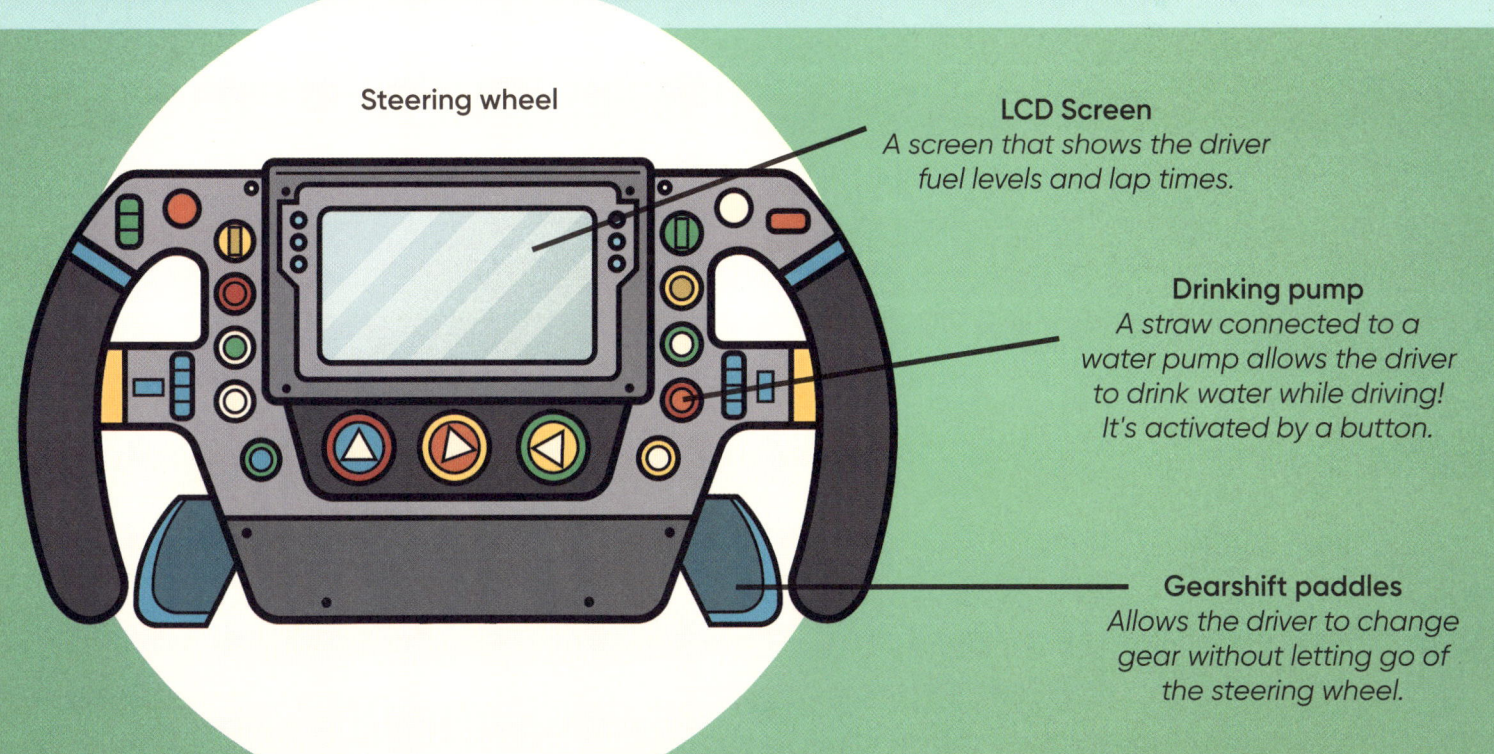

Steering wheel

LCD Screen
A screen that shows the driver fuel levels and lap times.

Drinking pump
A straw connected to a water pump allows the driver to drink water while driving! It's activated by a button.

Gearshift paddles
Allows the driver to change gear without letting go of the steering wheel.

STARTING LINE

Race day is finally here! The race teams and residents have filled the streets of Stemville, ready to see which team will be victorious. Frankie is feeling the pressure after her father, Poppa Thunderfoot, gives a pep talk. Wilbur and the Hardshells are feeling excited and surprisingly calm, trusting their good old logic and calculations.

YOU'RE NOT JUST DOING THIS FOR YOURSELF, IT'S FOR EVERY THUNDERFOOT THAT HAS GONE BEFORE YOU!

I'M GOING TO TRY MY BEST.

Reflex training

In F1, there are five starting lights. Between them all going on and turning off to start the race, there is a random delay. This is so that the drivers rely on their reaction time rather than knowing exactly when to go.

'Reaction boards' help train drivers' reflex skills and hand-eye coordination. They have to hit as many randomly lit lights as they can in 60 seconds!

The drivers are in position. They keep a close eye on the starting lights...

Step 1
The lights turn on one at a time...

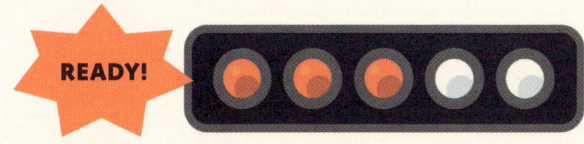

Step 2
There's a randomly timed delay of 0.2 to 3 seconds...

Step 3
The lights all turn off at once: the drivers step on the gas and GO!

The winning team is the one whose driver crosses the finish line first. This sounds simple, but lots can go wrong along the way...

THE NEED FOR SPEED

And they're off! Normal speed limits don't apply today. Frankie has her foot to the floor as she zooms off into an early lead. She's going so fast it feels like she's being pushed back in her seat! Wilbur is relaxing into the race, focusing on keeping up with the rest of the drivers.

G-force

Acceleration
Acceleration measures how quickly a car goes from 0 to 60 mph (97 km/h).

G-force

Gravitational force is known as G-force. It's the feeling in your belly that you get when you're on a rollercoaster. It's also what racing drivers experience when they move quickly or suddenly, like at the start of a race! Increased G-force can make your body feel heavier. It's like gravity giving you an extra push or pull in different directions.

Pass the tissues

G-force doesn't just pin you to your seat when you're accelerating. It also pulls your body forwards under braking. The pull of G-force is so strong, some F1 drivers have had tears sucked out of their watery eyes only to splash on the inside of their helmet's visor!

The top speed of regular modern cars is about 120 mph. The top speed in an F1 car is 231.4 mph!

GPS

A special GPS (global positioning system) in the car allows the rest of the team to monitor a car's speed, as split-second reactions are very important. GPS maps can help your team work out how your car is doing compared to others, and point out strengths and weaknesses.

GPS works by space satellites sending signals to electronic devices on Earth. These accurately pinpoint your device's location and provide directions to different destinations.

GPS is also used to pinpoint the drivers' race positions, which are then displayed on the leaderboard.

 STEMVILLE **BIG RACE**

LAP **5**/57

1	Nigel Honeybucket
2	Frankie Thunderfoot **FASTEST LAP!**
3	Wilbur Hardshell
4	Mica Cheever
5	Yuki Squeakio
6	Renée Stripe
7	Mo Plume

Pedal power

When drivers put their foot down on the accelerator pedal, the engine sucks in more air and fuel. This makes the car go faster.

Frankie steps on the accelerator and sets the record for the fastest lap so far.

WHAT A DRAG!

With the cars side by side, you can see the different shapes of each race car. These are not just for show – the teams behind each car have made many careful choices in their attempts to build the fastest machine possible, including size, shape and materials used.

D is for downforce

When a car moves, it travels through the air. We can't see it, but the air pushes down on the car, helping to stop it from flipping over. This downforce also allows more grip, so cars can go faster round corners.

... and drag

The air also produces friction as it pushes against the car, which is called drag. Annoyingly for racing drivers, drag can slow cars down.

Wings for the win!

Engineers have cleverly crafted wings to combat drag and increase downforce. These aren't wings to help cars fly like birds or planes, but carefully shaped parts set at angles that guide air over the car, lessening the amount of drag and increasing downforce for more grip.

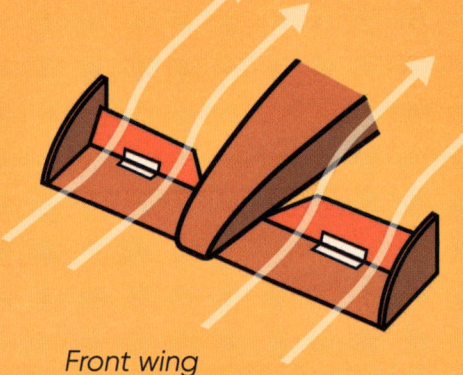

Front wing

Back wing

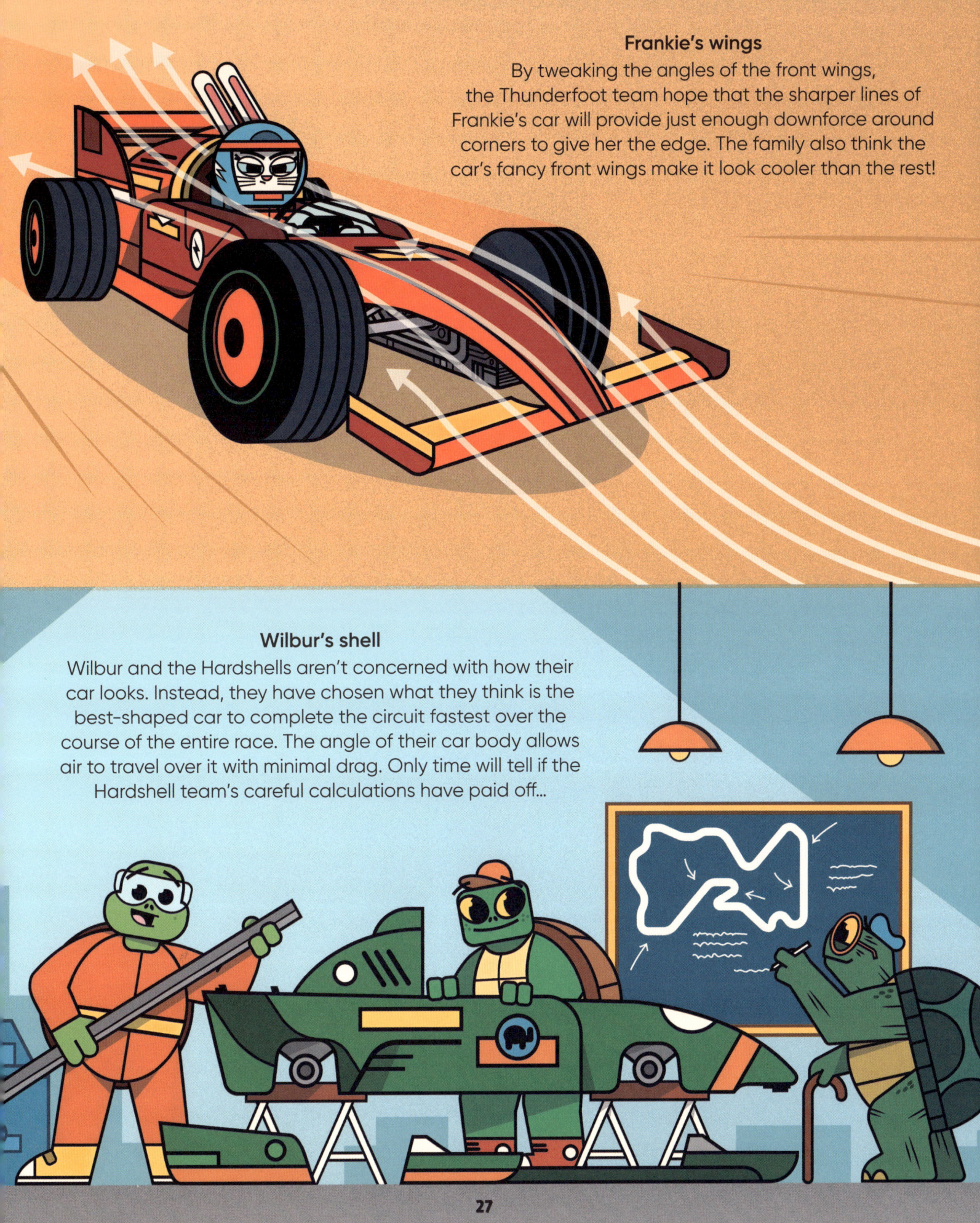

Frankie's wings

By tweaking the angles of the front wings, the Thunderfoot team hope that the sharper lines of Frankie's car will provide just enough downforce around corners to give her the edge. The family also think the car's fancy front wings make it look cooler than the rest!

Wilbur's shell

Wilbur and the Hardshells aren't concerned with how their car looks. Instead, they have chosen what they think is the best-shaped car to complete the circuit fastest over the course of the entire race. The angle of their car body allows air to travel over it with minimal drag. Only time will tell if the Hardshell team's careful calculations have paid off...

TERRIFIC TYRES

Oh no, it's started to rain! Thankfully, Frankie and Wilbur have chosen tyres that can cope with this mild shower. Nigel Honeybucket wasn't so lucky. He's ended up sliding off the track because his tyres don't have much grip. Sadly for the Honeybuckets, their race is over for another year...

I SHOULD HAVE CHECKED THE WEATHER FORECAST!

Slipping and sliding
When it rains, slick tyres are cooled by the water, which means that the sticky quality on them won't work. This can cause the car to aquaplane: in other words, spin and slide off the track!

Colour coding

Different tyres have colours on them so you can tell which is which. Around the tyre rim you'll see either red for the soft slick tyres, yellow for the mediums and white for the hard tyres. Green is used for medium and blue for wet.

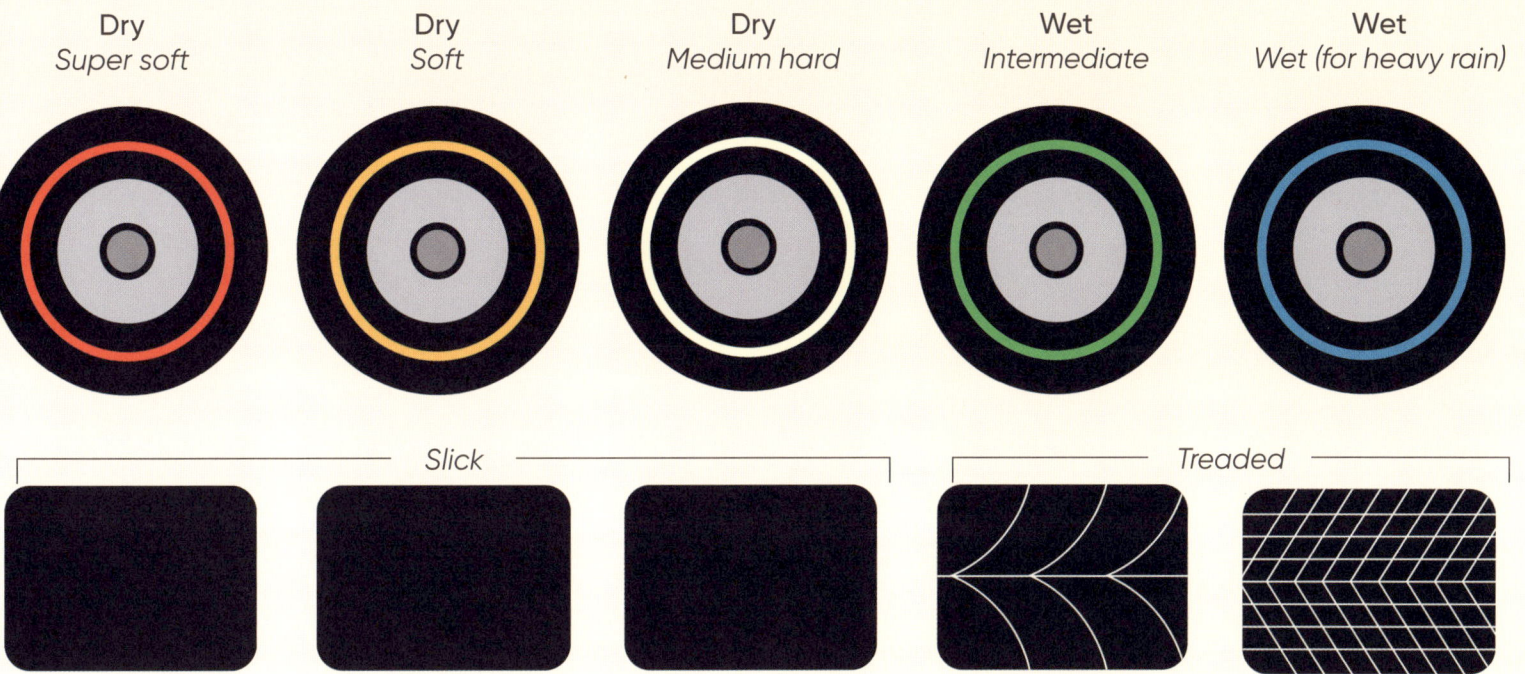

Dry	Dry	Dry	Wet	Wet
Super soft	*Soft*	*Medium hard*	*Intermediate*	*Wet (for heavy rain)*

Slick | *Treaded*

Dry weather tyres

In dry weather, F1 drivers use 'slick' tyres. These are smooth, treadless tyres with a sticky compound on them that ensures they get the biggest contact patch with the road to increase grip and traction.

Wet weather tyres

In wet weather, cars are fitted with tyres that have more grooves, and deeper grooves. This allows water to be moved from under the tyre when the rain is heavier. There are medium tyres for when the circuit is only a little wet, and wet tyres when it is really soaking and there may be puddles.

Yuki Squeakio pulls into the pit garage to change to wet weather tyres. Now she'll have enough grip to catch up with the other racers!

ENGINE POWER

Wilbur is concentrating very hard and taking the track by storm. He's taken his chance to overtake Frankie and race into the lead – this is a huge surprise! It's a good job the Hardshells built a powerful engine that's in tip-top condition, perfect for steaming ahead.

Engines are powered by petrol, which is very explosive. Petrol has 300 tiny explosions every second, so small amounts of petrol have to be used, sprayed into cylinders that are then lit by tiny sparks. The blast force pushes the pistol down.

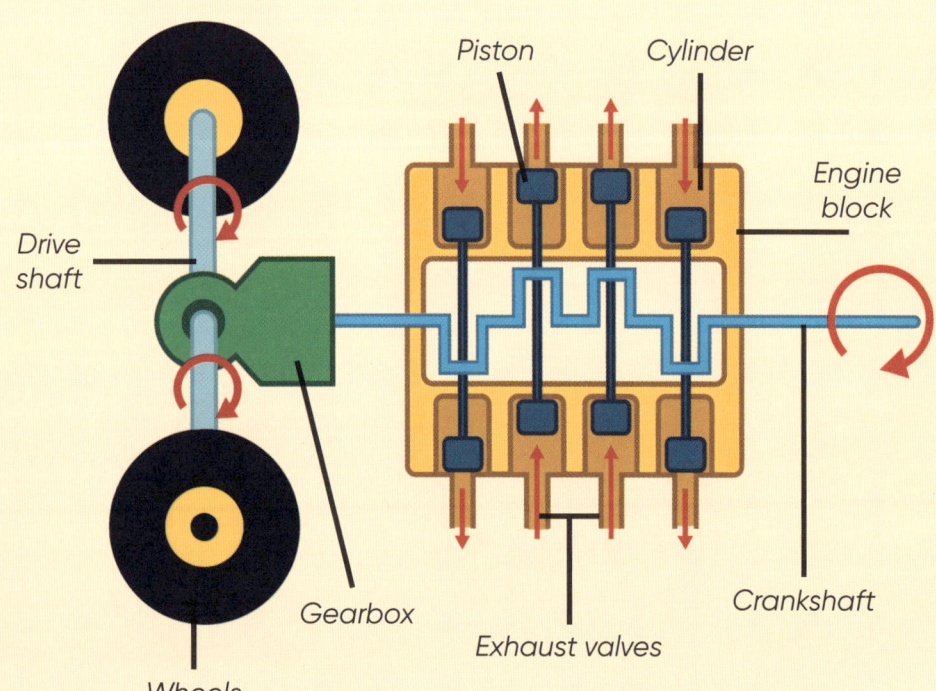

Piston

Cylinder

Engine block

Drive shaft

Gearbox

Exhaust valves

Crankshaft

Wheels

An engine goes through four stages, giving cars the power to move:

1. Air and fuel mix in the engine, as the piston (a metal disc) moves down.

2. The piston goes up, squishing the mixture, and making it hot and pressurised.

3. A spark plug ignites, causing a mini explosion and forcing the piston down.

4. After burning, the mixture is pushed out through the exhaust valve as the piston moves back upwards.

5. The pistons moving up and down spin the crankshaft they are attached to, which in turn spins the wheels through the gearbox.

Horsepower

The power of cars is often measured in something called 'horsepower' or 'hp'. This word was first used by a steam engine salesperson called James Watts. He wanted to explain to his customers how powerful the engine was compared to the strength of horses when pulling carriages was the main type of transportation at the time.

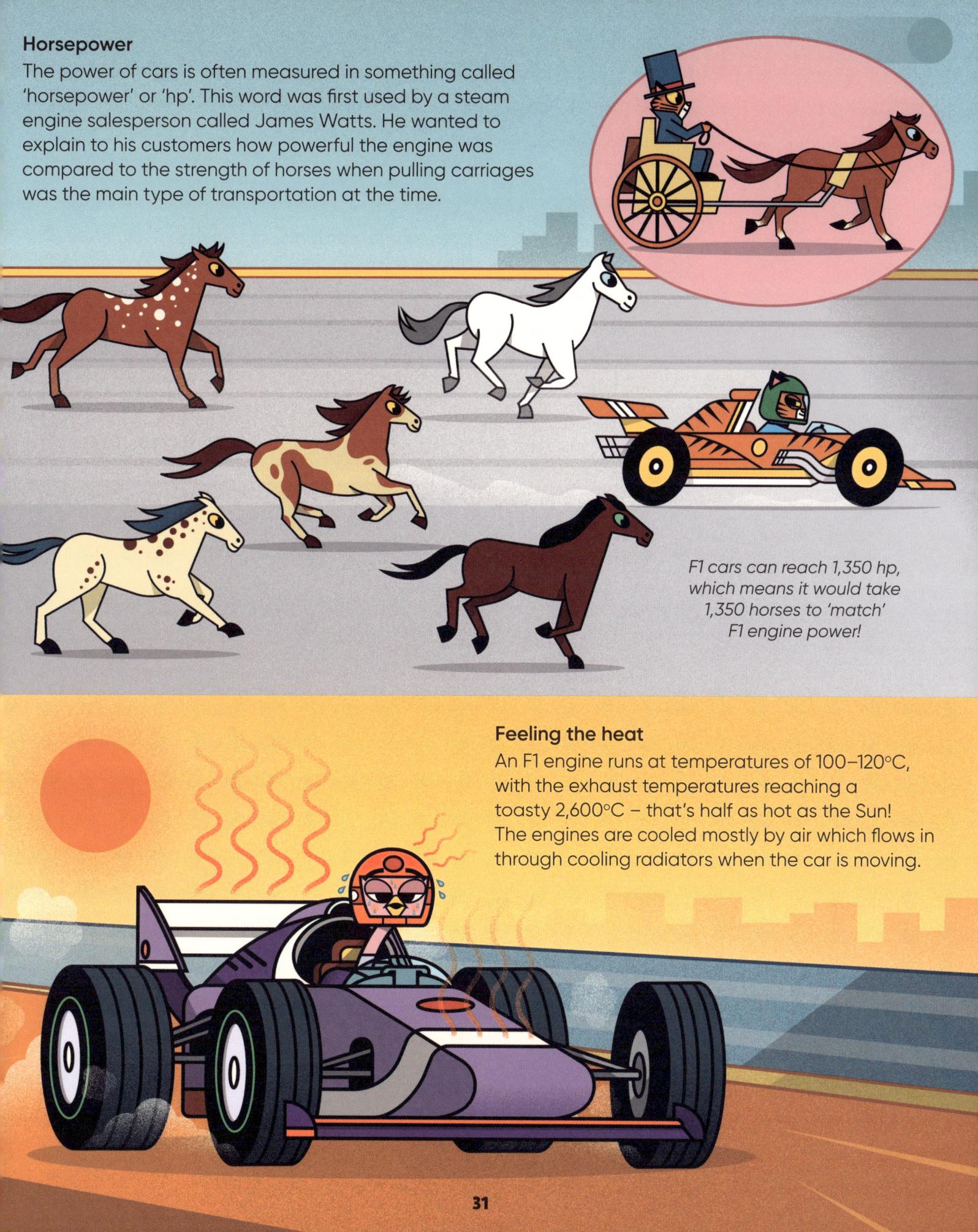

F1 cars can reach 1,350 hp, which means it would take 1,350 horses to 'match' F1 engine power!

Feeling the heat

An F1 engine runs at temperatures of 100–120°C, with the exhaust temperatures reaching a toasty 2,600°C – that's half as hot as the Sun! The engines are cooled mostly by air which flows in through cooling radiators when the car is moving.

DRIVING SKILLS

Oh no – just as Wilbur has taken the lead there appears to be a problem with his car. He is radioing the pit-stop team right now. Frankie seizes the opportunity to whizz past her opponent as Wilbur is slowing down. She opens the flap on her wing to speed up... And Frankie Thunderfoot is once again in the lead!

Overtaking
Overtaking (driving past another driver) is an important skill in car racing. And there are strict rules about it too. It must be done safely to ensure no cars are pushed off the track.

Slipping by
Getting right up close to a car in front of yours, in their 'slipstream', allows you to go faster when overtaking. The car in front is like a shield that protects yours from air resistance.

Timing it right
Drivers look at the cars ahead of them and try to spot anything that could signal it's the perfect time to overtake. They might notice that another car is braking too early, or that their tyres aren't coping well, and then go for it!

Magic wings

The wings on an F1 car act like a magic power-up tool. By pressing a button on their steering wheel, drivers can open a flap on the rear wing to increase speed by 10 mph. When the flap is up, it reduces drag. The driver can only use it in special zones on the circuit when near other cars in an attempt to overtake them. This makes for an exciting race!

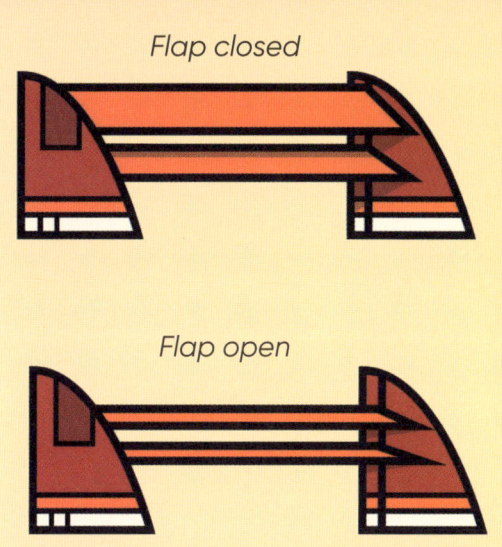

Flap closed

Flap open

Radio communication

Drivers have a button on their steering wheel that allows them to speak to their team, and their team to contact them mid-race. The driver uses a microphone and earpiece in their helmet, while the engineers and the rest of the team give feedback or pass on instructions from the pit.

NICELY DONE, FRANKIE! EVERYTHING IS LOOKING GOOD. WE SHOULD WIN THIS!

NON-STOP PIT STOP

Wilbur is feeling disheartened about losing his winning position. He drives to the pit lane and the Hardshell engineers get to work. But just because the car has stopped, it doesn't mean the action has! F1 pit stops only last around three seconds, so there's lots to get done in very little time...

Pit-stop team

More than 20 people are involved in an F1 pit stop. They practise hundreds of times to make sure everything runs smoothly. Everyone lines up in a particular order, ready to get their own job done. There's even a race version of a lollipop person who helps guide the driver into position!

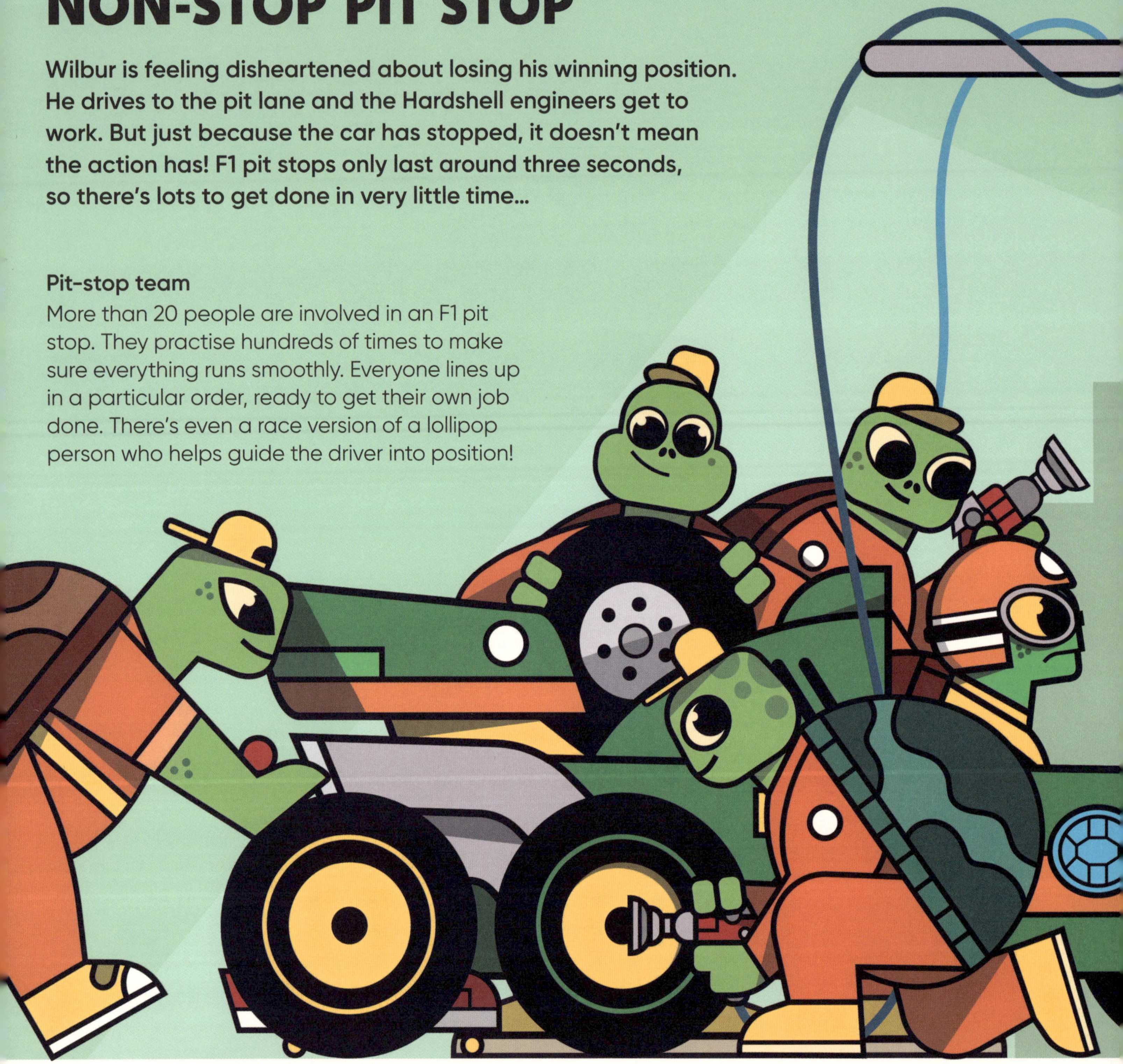

All change

Wheel changing is the fastest part of the pit stop. Wheel guns are used to swap wheels at incredible speeds. This 'gun' is a big air-powered wrench that undoes the wheel nuts. There are three mechanics to each wheel, meaning that there are 12 people just for tyre changing!

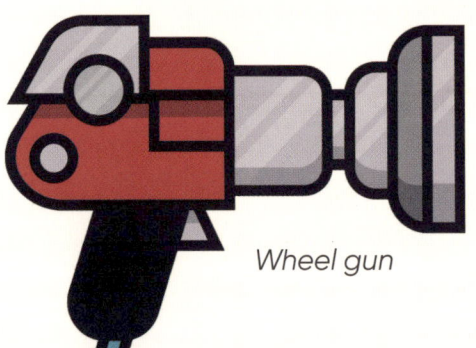

Wheel gun

The rain has stopped, so now Wilbur's car is fitted with soft slick tyres, which he and the Hardshell team hope will give him the speed to catch up with the rest of the drivers on the track...

GIVE ME A BRAKE!

Wilbur zooms back into the race. He overtakes Yuki Squeakio and is gaining on Mica Cheever as he rounds a tight corner. The Hardshell planning has paid off and Wilbur brakes at just the right time, rounding the corner with precision and ease.

Mica, however, has taken the corner too fast. He's spun off the track and damaged his car beyond repair! Mica is fine, but it looks like the race is over for the Cheever team...

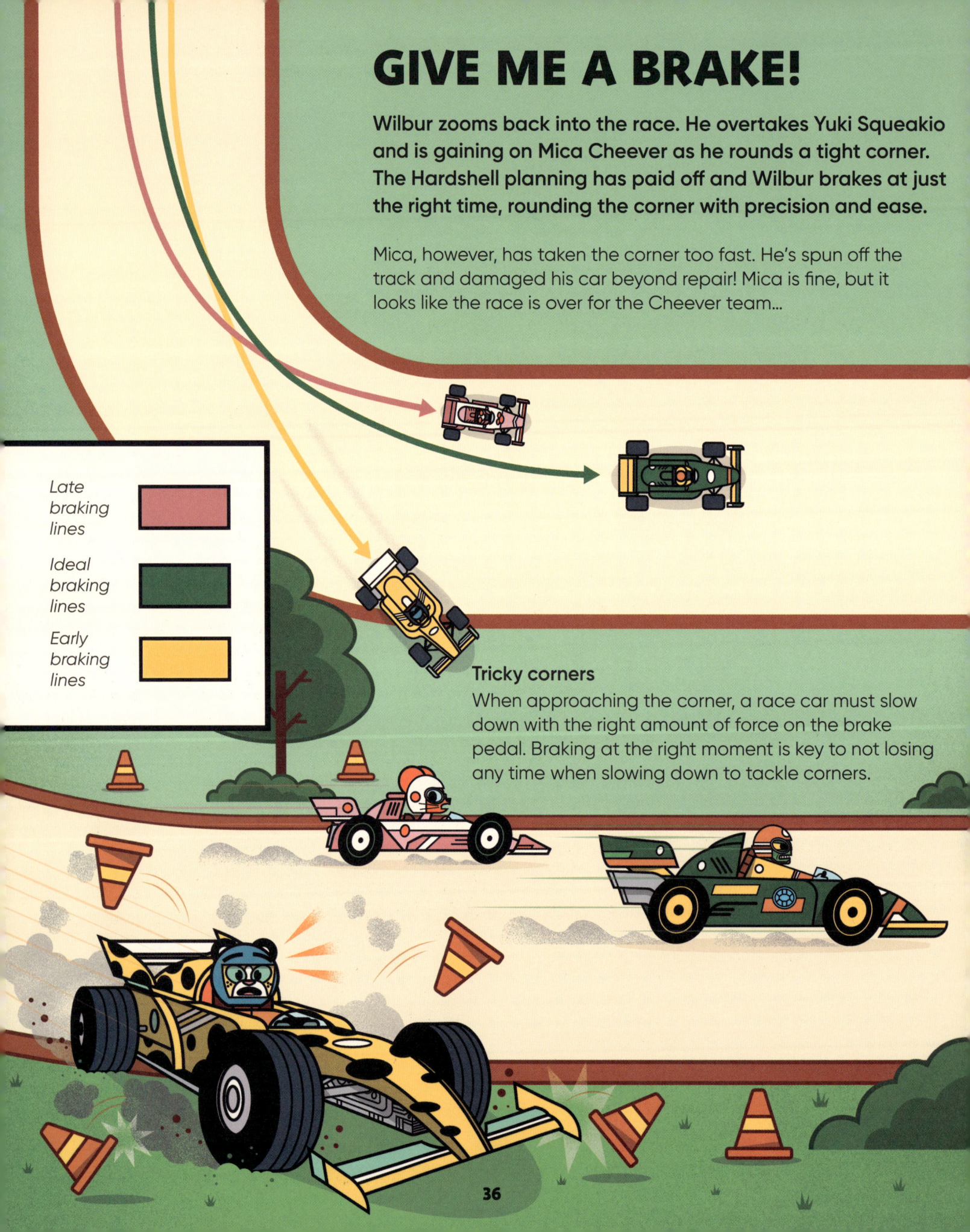

	Late braking lines
	Ideal braking lines
	Early braking lines

Tricky corners

When approaching the corner, a race car must slow down with the right amount of force on the brake pedal. Braking at the right moment is key to not losing any time when slowing down to tackle corners.

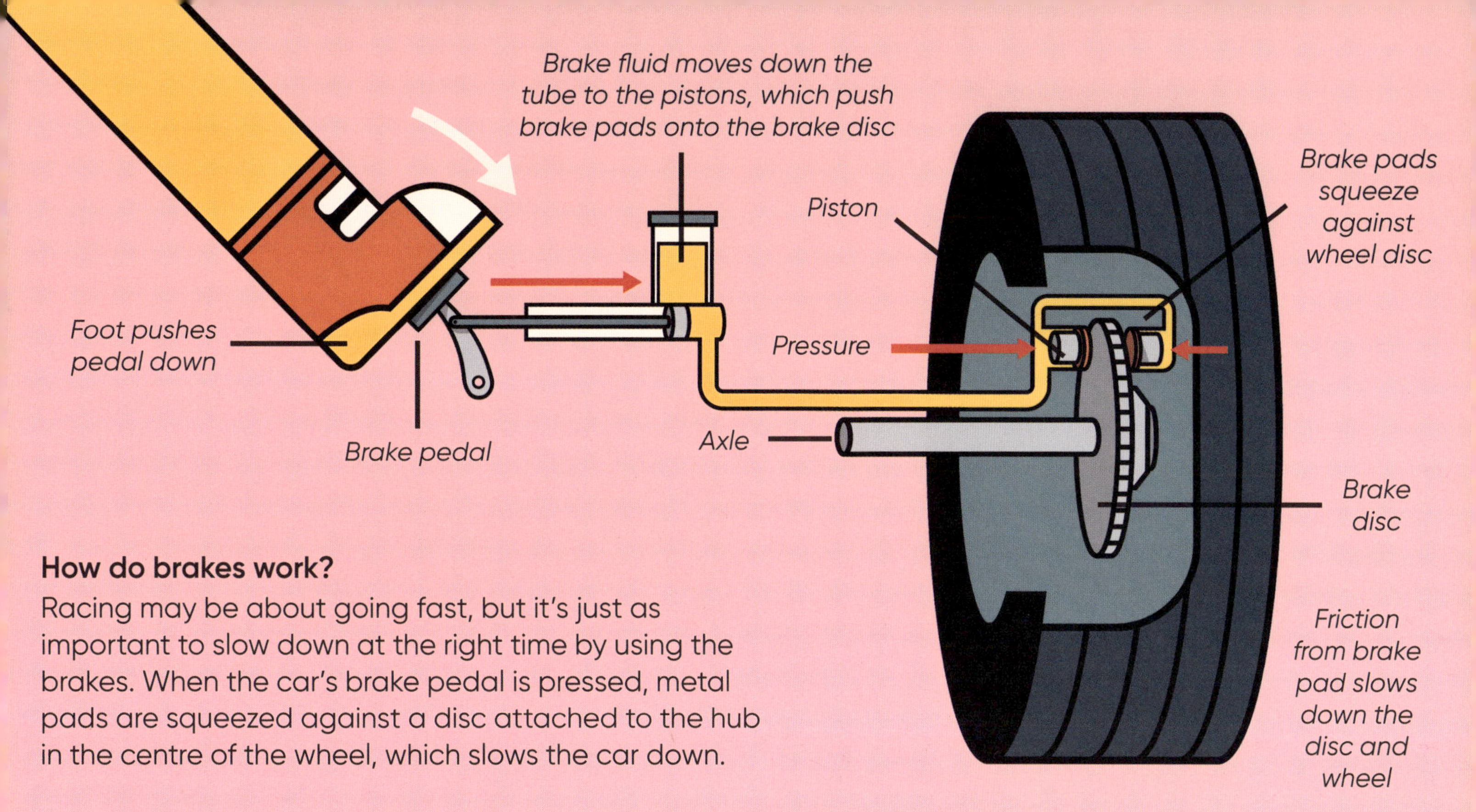

Brake fluid moves down the tube to the pistons, which push brake pads onto the brake disc

Piston

Brake pads squeeze against wheel disc

Foot pushes pedal down

Pressure

Brake pedal

Axle

Brake disc

Friction from brake pad slows down the disc and wheel

How do brakes work?

Racing may be about going fast, but it's just as important to slow down at the right time by using the brakes. When the car's brake pedal is pressed, metal pads are squeezed against a disc attached to the hub in the centre of the wheel, which slows the car down.

Safely out of the corner, Wilbur presses his boost button for a burst of extra speed!

Supercharge!

To get a supercharge of speed, drivers can boost their car with a special button. A flashing red light on the back of an F1 car signals that a driver is charging their battery so it's ready to boost.

SKIDDING AND CRASHING

Frankie feels like she is cruising to victory, until she spots Wilbur. He appears to be catching up – and fast! Distracted, Frankie takes a corner too wide. She spins off the track, hitting the barrier, and smoke rises from her car.

Hit the brakes!

If you are travelling fast and suddenly hit the brakes, the tyres lose their grip with the road surface. This loss of traction makes the car skid, meaning the driver loses control and the car can travel in an unwanted direction.

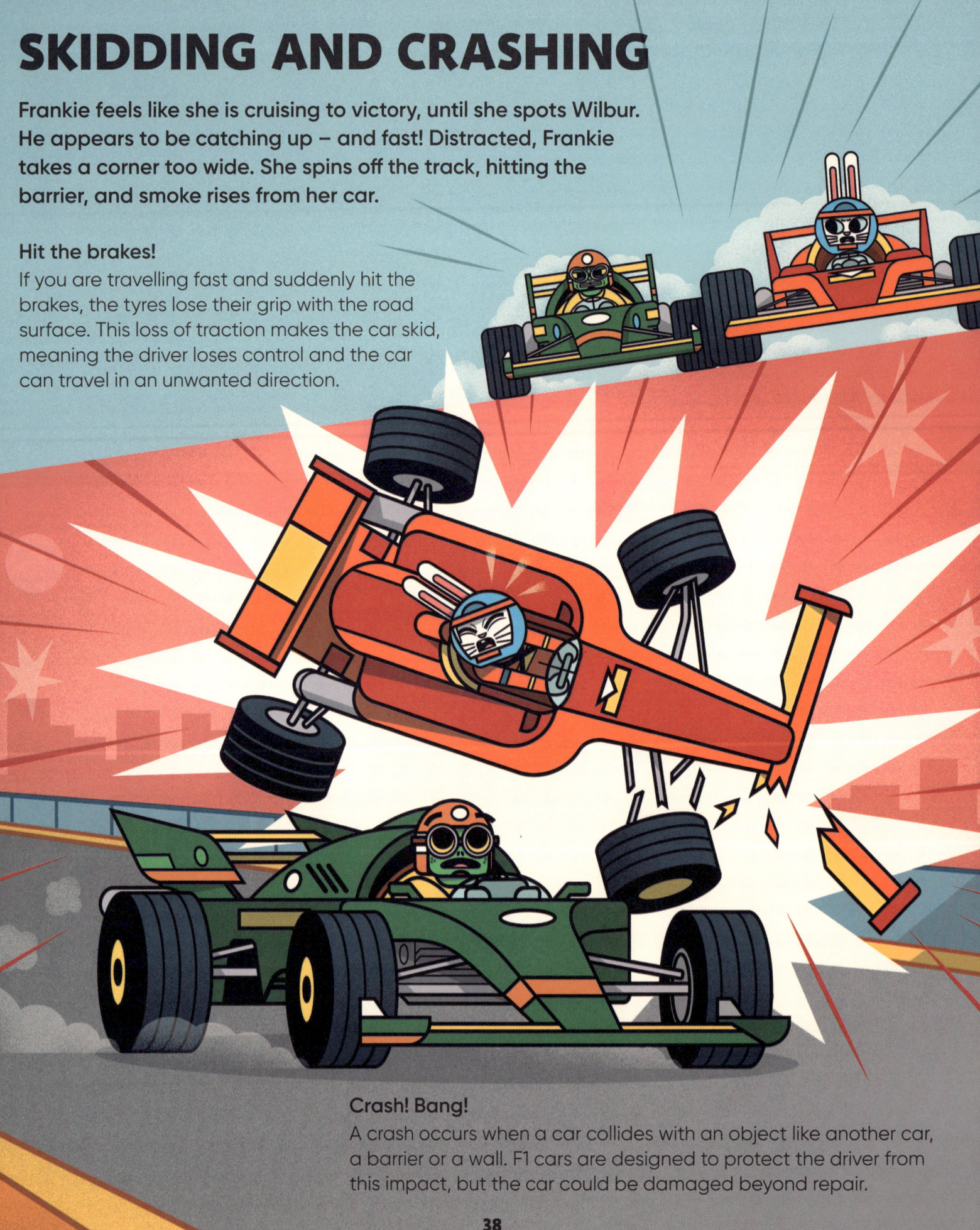

Crash! Bang!

A crash occurs when a car collides with an object like another car, a barrier or a wall. F1 cars are designed to protect the driver from this impact, but the car could be damaged beyond repair.

Safety first

Safety features to prevent crash injuries in F1 include:

A 'halo', a curved bar that surrounds the driver's head to shield them from injury if the car flips over.

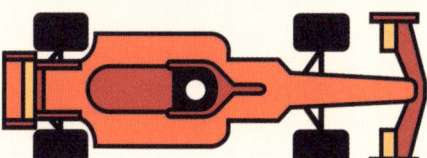

Fire-resistant carbon fibre helmets in case of flames from a crash.

Head rests and head and neck support to cushion the driver from getting hurt when going fast and turning sharply.

A removable steering wheel so drivers can easily get in and out of the car.

Belt up

Regular road cars have seat belts that go across the shoulder and waist and are fastened in the centre of the car. The F1 safety harness is far more secure, and has six belts that all meet in a metal buckle near the driver's belly button. They look more like the straps of a child's car seat. It helps keep the driver safe and reduces the effects of G-force.

Wilbur speeds past Frankie's crashed car into the lead, and he can see the finish line! But it looks like Frankie needs immediate help, and she's a long way from the ambulance unit. If Wilbur goes over to his rival, he'll be out of the race. What should he do?

EMERGENCY!

Wilbur decides to find a safe place to perform an emergency stop. A red flag is raised, and the race is paused. All the other drivers make their way to the pits. The crowd gasps as they watch Wilbur using his shell for protection as he helps Frankie out from her car.

Stop!

An emergency stop happens when a driver presses down really hard on the brake pedal with their foot, quickly bringing the car to a controlled stop.

POOR FRANKIE! THANK GOODNESS FOR WILBUR. BUT THEY NEED TO GET OUT OF THERE, AND FAST...

The residents of Stemville watch on nervously, not knowing whether Frankie will be OK...

41

FINISH LINE

The spectators can't quite believe their eyes. An exhausted Wilbur carries a grateful Frankie on his shell, and they cross the finish line together on foot. To their own surprise, they are not disappointed but thankful. The Thunderfoot and Hardshell families have forgotten their rivalry and are hugging in relief.

With Frankie and Wilbur back with their teams, the race can restart...

... And it looks like the tiniest racer is heading for the biggest day of her life! Yuki Squeakio is in the lead and her team are already starting to celebrate. But with Mo and Renée close behind, can Yuki cross the finish line first?

1	Yuki Squeakio	*Leader*
2	Mo Plume	*+1.230 secs*
3	Renée Stripe	*+1.567 secs*
-	Nigel Honeybucket	*DNF*
-	Mica Cheever	*DNF*
-	Frankie Thunderfoot	*DNF*
-	Wilbur Hardshell	*DNF*

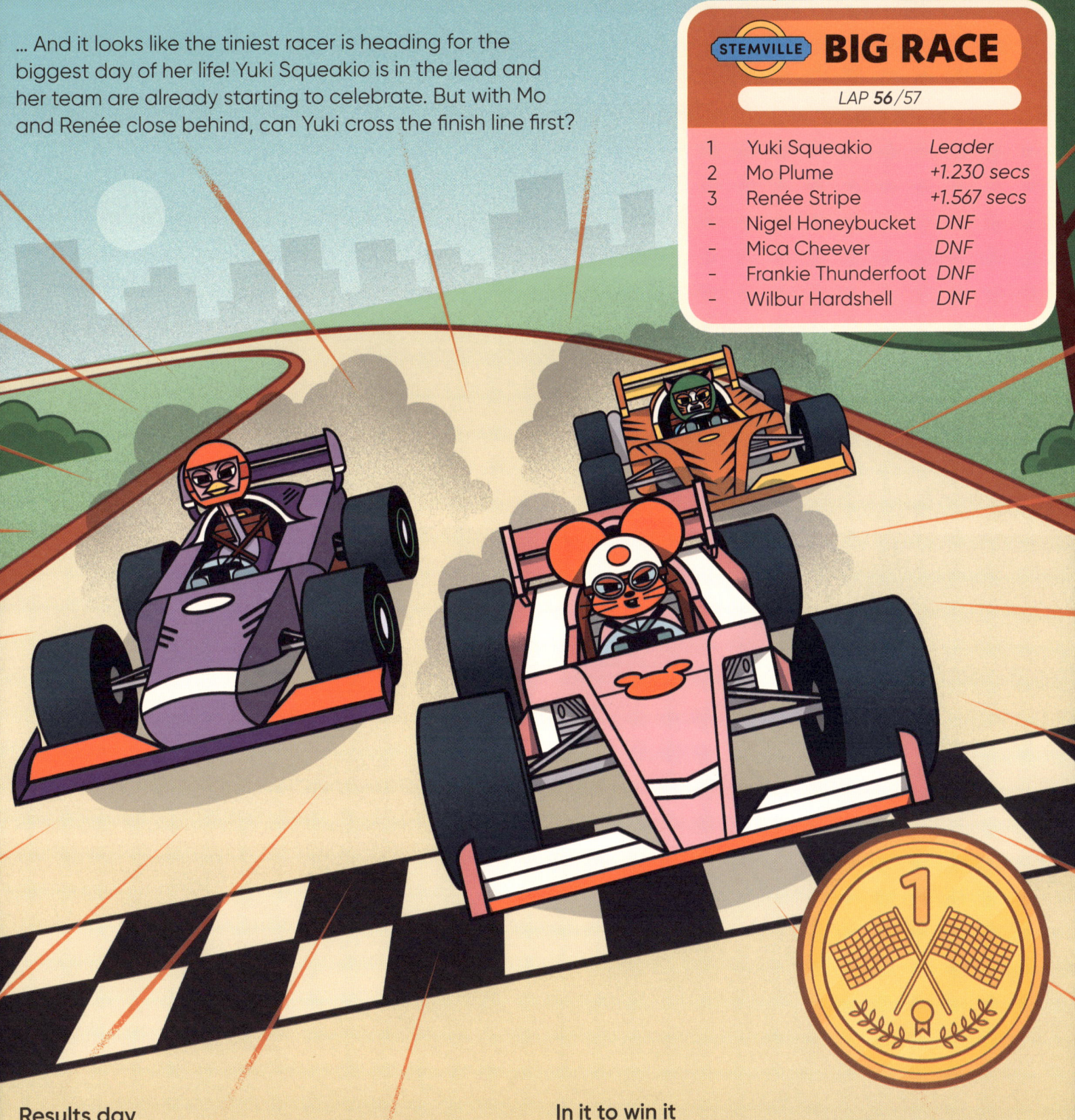

Results day

Once the winner has crossed the finish line, any remaining cars on the circuit continue to race. Their time is recorded as the number of seconds they are behind the winner. For cars who don't make it round, they receive a 'Retired', 'Disqualified' or 'Did Not Finish' (DNF) result, depending on the reason.

In it to win it

It was at the rainy Monaco Grand Prix in 1996 that a record was set for the fewest cars to finish a race. While 21 cars started, by the end only three cars crossed the finish line due to drivers losing control, crashing and collisions. This meant that all the drivers who finished the race got a medal!

BYE FOR NOW...

Everyone watches on as Yuki, Mo and Renée take their places on the finishing podium. Yuki's team squeak their congratulations – they managed to beat all the odds with a super lightweight miniature race car. There are also big cheers for Frankie and Wilbur. Despite their 'Did Not Finish' result they have amazed everyone with their bravery and newfound friendship.

The citizens of Stemville have learned that although sometimes things don't go as planned, you might end up with something even better instead. Three cheers for Yuki, and for Frankie and Wilbur – hip hip, hooray!

SLOW DOWN

Life can sometimes feel like you're living in the fast lane. Rushing to the next thing, trying to come first or getting things done as quickly as possible. Sometimes it's just as important to slow down, notice what is going on in the moment and enjoy the journey. Like Frankie, maybe everyone needs to be a little more Wilbur sometimes!